LET'S FIND OUT ABOUT

MARS

LET'S FIND OUT ABOUT

MARS

by DAVID C. KNIGHT

Pictures by DON MILLER

FRANKLIN WATTS, INC.
575 Lexington Avenue · New York, N.Y. 10022

Copyright © 1966 by Franklin Watts, Inc.
Library of Congress Catalog Card Number: AC66-10159
Manufactured in the United States of America
by The Moffa Press, Inc.
1 2 3 4 5

LET'S FIND OUT ABOUT

MARS

6

Of all the planets, Mars is the one people
  wonder about the most.
More words have been written about Mars
  than all the other planets put together.
Long, long ago, people saw Mars in the sky.
Some of them even worshiped it.

SATURN

JUPITER

URANUS

Mars is the planet you can see most clearly
   from Earth.
It is a part of the Solar System, just as
   Earth is.
There are nine planets in the Solar System.
All the planets travel around the Sun in
   paths called orbits.
Earth is the third planet from the Sun.
Mars is farther away.
It is the fourth planet from the Sun.

EARTH

MERCURY

VENUS

SUN

MARS

NEPTUNE

PLUTO

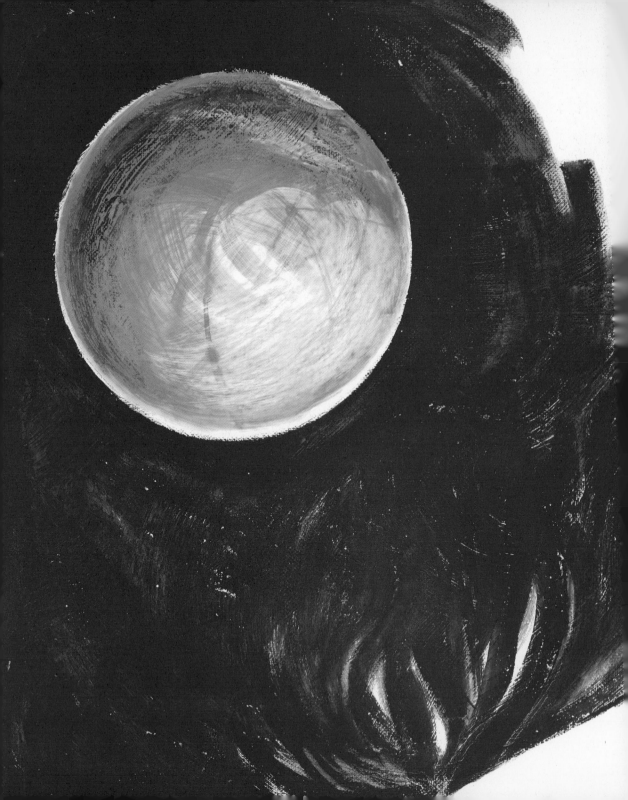

Mars is sometimes called the Red Planet
    because it shines with red and orange light.
But Mars does not shine with light of its
    own.
Mars gets its light from the Sun, just as
    Earth does.

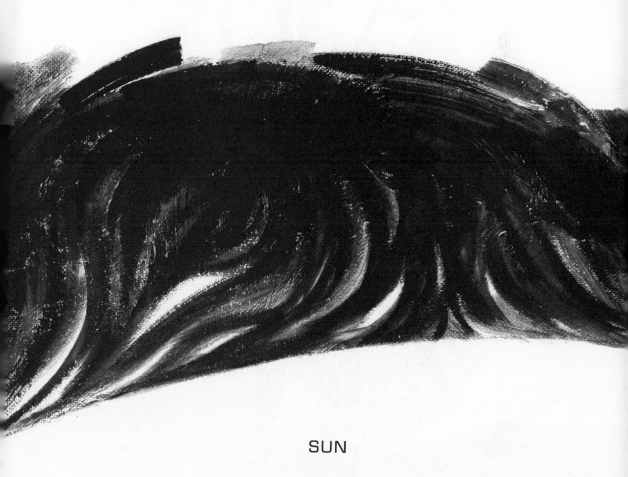

SUN

Who gave Mars its name? — the Romans who
   lived long ago.
Its red color reminded them of blood and
   war.
So the Romans named the planet Mars, after
   their God of War.

When you look up at the sky at night, Mars
    is one of the brightest things you can see.
It is even brighter than Jupiter, the biggest
    planet in the Solar System.
But Jupiter is farther away from us than
    Mars.
It is the fifth planet from the Sun.

Of course, some nights you cannot see Mars
  at all.
It is below the horizon — the edge of the
  Earth.
When Mars is close to the horizon at sunrise,
  it may be called the Morning Star.
When it is close to the horizon at sunset,
  Mars may be called the Evening Star.

17

Both Mars and Earth go around the Sun
in the same direction.
Some years Earth comes closer to Mars than
other years.
How close do we get to Mars?
The closest we get to Mars is about 35
million miles..
That is when scientists can study Mars the
best.

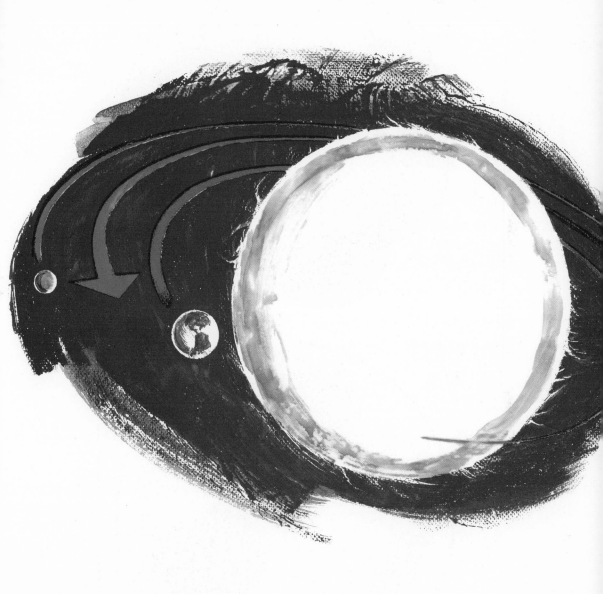

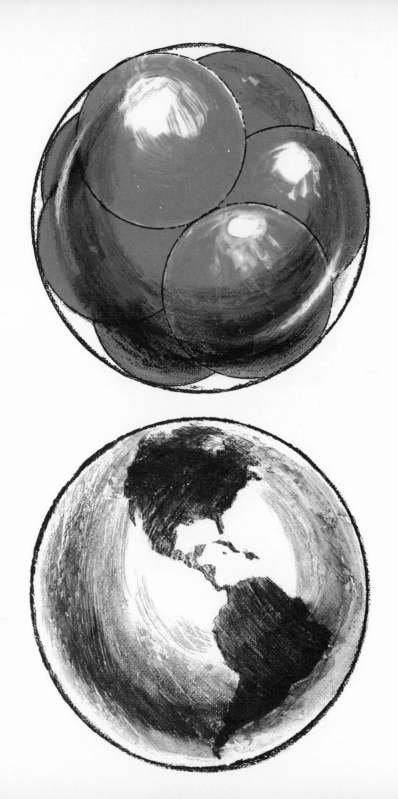

Mars is small compared to Earth.
It would take seven planets the size of Mars
to make one Earth.

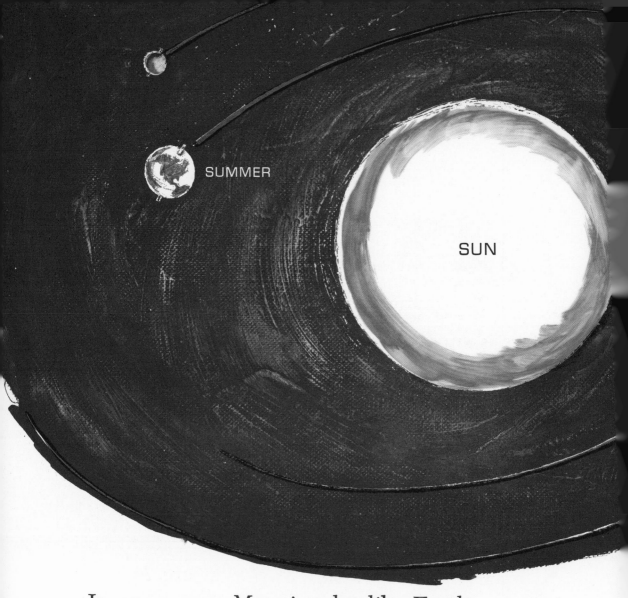

SUMMER

SUN

In some ways Mars is a lot like Earth.
Mars travels through space about 15 miles
    every second, just a little faster than Earth.
Earth and Mars spin like tops in about the
    same time.

WINTER

This gives both of them days that are 24
hours long.
Earth and Mars are each tilted toward the
sun at about the same angle.
This gives both of them seasons — spring,
summer, fall, and winter.

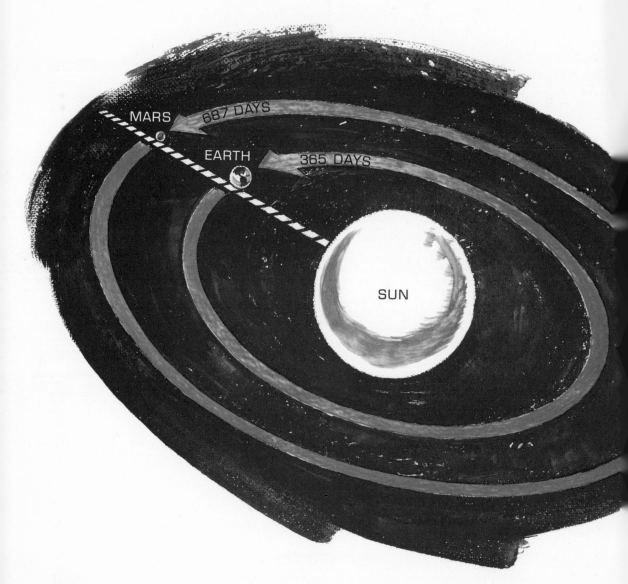

In some ways Mars isn't like Earth at all.
Mars takes almost twice as long to go around
  the Sun.
This means that a year on Mars lasts almost
  twice as long as a year on Earth.
It also means Mars has longer seasons.
On Mars summer lasts almost twice as long
  as it does on Earth.

26

Mars has two moons instead of just one like Earth.

They are very tiny worlds called Phobos and Deimos.

You could walk clear around Phobos in about 12 hours.

Deimos is even smaller than Phobos.

Scientists have always been curious about
Mars.

Of all the planets, they think Mars may be
the one with some kind of life on it.

But even with big telescopes, astronomers
cannot find out much about Mars.

It is too far away.

So scientists dreamed of the day when it
would be possible to send a spacecraft to
Mars to take pictures.

That day came in 1964 when a huge rocket
boosted a tiny spacecraft into space.

29

This famous spacecraft was Mariner 4.
It flew as far as 325 million miles through
    space before it reached Mars in 1965.
The long trip to the Red Planet took more
    than 7 months.
Mariner flew by Mars and went on into
    farther space.
Its camera took 21 pictures of Mars and sent
    them back to Earth by radio.

When the scientists saw Mariner's pictures,
    they were surprised.
The pictures showed many deep holes called
    craters, just like those on the Moon.
The scientists had not thought there were
    craters on Mars.
The craters did not seem to be worn down
    by any rain or rivers or water of any kind.

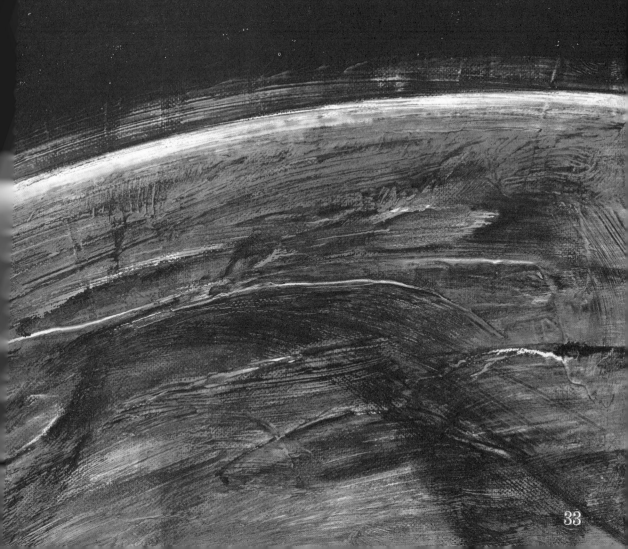

Mars seemed to be a dead world, like the
  Moon.
The kind of life we know on Earth needs
  water.
But there seems to be no water on Mars.

In the years before Mariner's famous trip,
    writers liked to make up stories about
    Mars.
Not much was known about Mars.
It seemed like a mysterious place.
The writers would write stories about little
    green men, and strange monsters, and
    cruel robots.
Some even wrote about Martians coming to
    conquer Earth.
Of course, they were only stories — no one
    believed them.

35

36

But many people did believe one story about
   Mars.
It is the story of the Martian canals.
It goes like this:
Almost a hundred years ago, some
   astronomers thought they saw straight
   lines on Mars through their telescopes.
The man who first saw them named them
   canals.
The lines seemed too straight to be rivers.
They looked more like canals, which are
   ditches for water dug by people.
So it was thought that there were people on
   Mars.

The story went on this way:

Mars was losing its water.

It was drying up.

As Mars grew drier and colder, people moved closer to the equator.

But the only water was at the poles where the frozen ice caps were.

So the Martians built canals to make the water run down to the equator when the ice melted in the spring.

Then the Martians could have water to drink.

But things got worse for the Martians.
The planet got colder and drier.
The water at the poles ran out.
Soon there was no more water in the canals
    for the people to drink.
One by one the brave Martian people died
    until none were left.
That is the way the story ends.

Today only a few people still believe that there are canals on Mars.

Scientists studied Mariner's pictures very hard, but they could not seem to see any real canals.

Yet they have not given up hope that canals might be there, or that there is some kind of life on Mars.

To find out for sure, astronauts will have to go to Mars.

It will be many years before men can be
sent to Mars.

Our scientists will have to solve many
problems first.

Enough food and water and fuel will have
to be taken along for a trip that will take
months.

A way will have to be figured out for a safe
landing on Mars.

If astronauts land and stay on Mars, they
will have to have supplies sent to them
from Earth.

And scientists will have to figure out how to
get the astronauts home again.

When the astronauts land on Mars, they will
  have to bring tanks of air with them.
People need air to breathe or they will die.
Scientists know that the Martian air is very
  thin.
They think it is mostly a gas people cannot
  breathe.
Wherever astronauts go on Mars, they will
  have to carry their air supplies around
  with them.

Scientists know that the force of gravity is weaker on Mars than it is on Earth.

This means that things are lighter on Mars than they are on our planet.

If an astronaut weighs 150 pounds on Earth, he would weigh only about 57 pounds on Mars.

He would be able to jump about three times higher on Mars than he could on Earth.

Because Mars is farther away from the Sun,
the Red Planet is quite a bit colder than
Earth.

When the sun goes down on Mars, it freezes
every night.

If astronauts go out at night on Mars, they
will need heating systems built into their
space suits.

When enough scientists can get to Mars, they
will build a station there.
They will have important scientific jobs to
do.
Biologists will study any signs of life there.
Geologists will dig into the ground to see
how Mars is made.
Astronomers will study the other planets and
the distant stars through their telescopes.

After many years, men from Earth might
    build cities on Mars.
They may build them underground.
Families of these men will go there to live.
The Red Planet will no longer be a
    mysterious place.
It will be home.